Noctilucent

Noctilucent

Melissa Buckheit

Shearsman Books

First published in the United Kingdom in 2012 by
Shearsman Books
50 Westons Hill Drive
Emersons Green
Bristol BS16 7DF

Shearsman Books Ltd Registered Office
30–31 St. James Place, Mangotsfield, Bristol BS16 9JB
(this address not for correspondence)

http://www.shearsman.com/

ISBN 978-1-84861-215-0

Contents

For Rebecca

and

for Olga

Noctilucent

there's the desert beyond them that I try to keep housed from
no thin flesh there no coursing fluid no thought

—Alice Notley

My life
    by water
        Hear—

—Lorine Niedecker

Noctilucent

In speaking of *kyanós,* cyano

                      blue, a dark-blue mineral in designations
of certain bluish salts and minerals,
                           of cyanide, cyanic

    the blueness of skin
                    cyan
    the blueness of sky

                      whose greenish-blue is like water
breathed in, supplants air

        (my) cyanosis
                  condition in which the skin appears
  blue from no oxygen in the blood

                  Blue the blue of painted Greek boats, blue

mercury light
             alive   with the kindling of moths,

                           shy, shining
in the night

  little noctilucae   not marred in their bioluminescence, night-

glow (if bugs)

making marine phosphorescence,

                                       like love

Latin moon-lantern, Japanese moon-

lanterns strung orange

for the night-
          walk to a lover's door   preceding electric blue
                                       lights of the city
from space

    nights are illuminated by noctilucent clouds, waves, beaches
                                   and celestial orbs

   migrations of aquatic plants whose cyan flight
                           is mutable change in light,

   dark (the homes) we make glowing in

other bodies

                                      our lovers

asleep   (inside us)

Suffering

This isn't the answer. The answer is my hand on the table, saying
what we thought privacy was, on your forehead cupping the
temple where the fine hairs begin. What origin begins with
hair, the tenderest movement out, ends with bodies lining graves,
an inability to pronounce the phonemes of your now foreign
language. The language itself, an answer. The woman isn't
answering the phone, the woman isn't answering anyone. The
woman isn't. The woman is chemically altering from the
moment she is ignited. The woman is a girl. My palm across
your temple, your eyes which follow me as I remove it.
Tied to a tree isn't the answer. Tied to the back of a truck
isn't the answer, as it moves over miles, isn't the cold hospital room,
isn't "you're not my daughter anymore and you'll never be
my son." This answer is evolving, this poem isn't, recall to me
the names inscribed on sheets, almost almost. Your palm
as it cups my temple, covering the left eye, the language itself.
This isn't a wave as it takes a whole island, then buries the island
beneath the island.

Archipelago

Who would hear you? Home is aside the silence. Adored, unadorned. Purple-pink striations as inside a child. Butterfly. Two lips. I am speaking of quartz. Two women cross the damp road, ambling up the street. Both in pants, one coat. Enter into one car. As they close the door, a squirrel loops past, disappearing around the wheel of the tire. Sun becomes visibly brighter, brighter at high altitude like a mirror shown white.

Did it rain — just a few minutes ago. A certain safety in prose satisfies. Even as we speak. Soon the sun comes out again, and later, the solace of gray I remember like childhood, mood so rare even the storm's yellow leaves will not allow it. They fall, dark.

A solid day without interruption save the parabolic rumble of bus. All four directions. If one thing appears, another may continue it. As a group of islands, if you circle them, eventually you will begin again at a group of islands. The same schema. Always earth changes, moving us, clouds on a continuous chart. Now waves push and shift; one island a bit more north than we could remember. *Paros,* liquid green mound & dry sands. A group of islands, a chief sea. *Pelagic shell* adored, unadorned. Of the sea, of the sea. Master. I have. Forgotten. Where were we going?

Let the sun warm you. On a bed in the open light. Late August, but it's September. Fluvial. Entered by a lavender plant. At the base of a line, intersecting the light and you. Cool air, it's pleasurable. Please from *pelagos*. Related words, placate— Any jar is an open sea. The broken one meant for transporting water to the home. Bottles, as if I can't say they are women. The sun goes "in". *Domus* means "not interference". The waves at sight.

Datura

A flower not diurnal
                almost poisonous,

    vivid in the half-dark
                of opposing particles—

        a cushion with the light
behind it
                    your silhouette

            below my limbs as sleep

        breaks away

    I call you

    to the corner of the room   where the shelf
                            of sea begins

                            mid-air

Epis

the first moment I slipped inside
we were born

hand who shines and shines
reflecting

your soul a vine
herding
cosmic string

shyest delight
shyest fire
obliterates

always sleep
in the sleeve of my collarbone

when you speak
you speak
poetry's rise

Sappho knew your name

two hundred stars
all nameless
evening's

call me with the knife
of your tongue
flower

no snake
but one tended in the temple

baby again named

in the forest the fruit of your nipples

Eve remembers

Hildegard

In what lairs
we cached our nimble fingers—
secret salve of a sister's voice,
liquid, repetitive, chill like night.
No ice but stones encasing us,
rhythmic weight of Candlemas,
aria, matins.

I kept my thirds hidden on rich paper,
needlepoint, whale-inked.
What passion engraved
should arise and I flush, what
floating heart, murmur
of a lover, Him / my sisters,'
a vacuum to which I faint?

We all faint. No remarkable mind
tethered above but our own breast
now bound low. Below

~

ecstasy of a third   was an herbalist, medicinal

(lived) in a box

was an animal's intestine, on fire

Demotics

quanta surpassed by penumbra

driven mad, the sea

       its repeated horizon steering straight

  down the canyon   coral reef senita who blooms at night

                    monitor of

ocotillo curvature

             where have you gone

                        my memory is an emission

      photograph

               rapid ball of light her skull lasting

a yellow glow of sodium means atoms are relaxing

        the jackrabbit allows a fear of sand

in bed time is transferable and small

could become a tremor

        a length of cloud with another

jelly-like

        the pelvis appears
               among deep-sea vent

      combing the water for
our symbolon

conifer and magnolia consumed before desiccation

                                 in a mud bed
      cousin to the diatom our dimorphic

   we all live at the river
              the moon reduces to tides

Dune-field
        to which we may attach a quay

    oscillation for boat
            or the desert's

                all indivisible energy exists

Raga

minimal amount of music cut up

to its ecliptic   pleasure

as the neutrino flies   constantly through my flesh

re-arrange surrender

Pheromone
                    the honeybee signals danger from

    a kiss

                            after fight or flight
        my anabasis

                                        kelp-forests and

olive-green limpets, petrel, pelagic

                          atoll, lipstick
                              pixie, fairy puke—

        night-aquifer

water is why
　　　　the epiphytes or guest plant

　　paints chartreuse over stones, cedar, hand-

rails　　I hold on for dear life
　　　　　　　　marriage

the rarer just offshore arroyo

as perilune swallows

sea-level

sockeye-less salmon

dead or diverted in sleep

what you don't know,
quiet underneath

too wet for trees

fungi people / epiphyte
keep my sexless sex safe

humans hate darkness

        to inspire people about the deep

  ocean, we had to light it was a boundary

                  as he shut off the lamp
                        blurred my flagellum

Post-Modern Epithalamion

Love,
            the blade of grass you kicked up as we swung
high on Tower Hill. It spun past my eyes, a vision
in wet, alive. Whitman loved young grass and boys.
I love you. What is the secret
                              of language, what is secret
      the fragment of Sappho a poem still incomplete but
how private for what's missing. A lover? Sexier. Language
conveyed to another where both are absent. Return
not like Odysseas after
too many years, but real and invoked. Like O'Hara coming home
with his Verlaine, caught for a moment with Billie,
                                    but alone
      I'm secret, spoken against your ear
                              not a dream or lament,
but poetry.   Put your tongue against mine. This

      is not a vow, but what is the secret
of love?   It's alive.

Polis

If it's parallel to Greece, they are building a subway system, a *métro* to reach all over Athens. Loosening the stones of the Plaka, I might cry. Tunneling deep into the city, a (warm) animal who has never been asleep, only accumulating layers, rings, pleasure upon pleasure, *domus* on *domus*. Suddenly it's dark, you enter, the train is slow, creeps before a sudden surge through the sheath under the city, rails cut out. They've walled off in glass or plexiglas markers and maps of *domi*, I pretend they are (Roman) (some are) only seen from the entrance of each age, horizontal terra half-walls, white stone, form compounding form, split diagonal running headlong into 300 years later. This time just a slit of rubble sandwiched for the eye. Kiss me while we pass them—our homes, destinations, entrances. Beneath the light shoals of a small inlet caressing Cape weeds, marshland, thicker salt than any Mediterranean name, the same *métro* beneath surf, sun-reflected wave. An archipelago can be made of sand only two meters wide, by noon it has receded like salt flung over a boat to clarify. Eyes to the plexiglas. A wife who rarely strayed from her square house sleeps, powdered bones and stone, vacuum-packed air separated by a line of glass. We may live in the shoal, hours to float salt-weight, breathing mirror under sea.

Lotus

In this dream, the lotus is faced down

tucked beneath the fading sun

or maybe floating in mid-air, engraved
                          on a yellow and turquoise silk.

When I sat today, a great eye kept appearing
                          in the field of my mantra

long black eyelashes & no iris, just a pupil

as in E.'s class I sit below a great

lotus-flower, primary-colored
                          which floats above my head

as we turn to face the white wall.

In my dreams, I fly by extending my legs back,
                          and balancing my weight
through my waist.
                    I never flew as a child. I don't
think I ever floated.

                          People had tied themselves

to a wrist, a child on a leash,

except I was leading.

I was the child.

Would you lie about exiting the birth canal,

                              coccyx-first? No,

I don't remember the obstetrician reaching

              into her gut and pulling me away

from the pressure, gravity, through

the laceration. Yes,

                              she was a woman-doctor. She left
a late-summer barbecue to deliver

a slick baby through the salted fluid.

She only anesthetized the spine,

                              so we were both awake,
wakened from a dream, the lotus

                    tilted up, 30 degrees, stirrups wide &

how she wouldn't dilate; yes, we were breathing

I sneezed and our hearts stopped in unison,

                         only a second, then

my crown peeking through the sticky pink eye,

we cried.

As If I Were Conceived in Her Diorama

1

i the daughter face a window outside this house. if
you place a chair a foot behind the panes, the
audience will see me, unmoving, the lip of the stage
a parallel line to their bodies troused in yellow light.
each leg an isosceles through the endpoint to the
midpoint. the very back of my head, soft spot in
skulls of infants, is the vanishing point

2

she is my mother's sister. when her head appears,
the brain merges   green squares of light in the
circuits and neurotransmitters. face as blank as
green glass or my own i never know. the green
words for the frame bury the distinction of bodies.
if i am angry it is because *someone has dialed my
number*: *juniper, goggles, bladderwrack, bottles,
laminaria* frame the blackness of a room where the
frame is a black perimeter indistinguishable from
the room

3

sometimes you call up someone else's aphasia, a
taste like raw silk in the mouth, several ideas of
yourself consuming the clothes worn all summer—
linen pants and coats, capris and shells, shell button-
down shirts and side-slit skirts. then to crouch in the
box of green light, nude, letting the shutter's eye
lick the light of my torso; curves conjugated
guttural sounds

4

i whose daughter of a man whose words i do not
hear fall behind the parallel lines intersecting
our bodies' frames. drive in the car stage left, no
dialogue for movement. on the couch center as he
focuses on some point in the rafters, what
Stanislavsky taught, empathizing with some
spectacular childhood trauma or tv. i am
perpendicular to him and that lighted box of energy
whose particles disperse his eyes, a wavelength i
cannot seem. i not the daughter to a man crying
under the kitchen table in shell shock, who rapes my
aunt in his bed, a square almost-windowless room,
10 feet down the hall

5

the afterimage of the bulb on the eye is really the
eye itself, accretive cone a mirror through relation
on the far side of the box. the bulb is a dead white
hiding blue glass holding dead white the waves
emanate through. cone of heat enters my pelvis, red
clementine of capillaries, cage from spectrum, slice
gone out. spiraling of ribs, heart religion to the bulb
of the eye obliterated by blood

6

sometimes you call up your own aphasia. a square
of window sluiced with water. you can see
reflection in the floor—to sleep in the supply
cabinet or under library tables, reading the words of
novels taken from their original language across a
bridge of throats not yet cut by knives, *willful
destruction of her texts*

7

bits of statuary plowed up in a field, carbon-made
objects collected and assembled to exhibit circular
patterns in large public spaces, mildew in pipes and
bath-drains, a green gel photographed in the dark
over a frame with a spotlight behind the body as the
horizon, the waves of Odysseas' black curls, the
Desert Sidewinding Adder, photosensitive plants
and native chameleons indistinguishable from
habitat, how the ocean begins, Sappho's dewy
syllables

        unearth she endecka

                syllabics

                      hand-tongue-thumb

    to lotus

Like the Sea Is Empty and Full

She sends a bottle
                    of seawater

wrapped in a skirt smelling of her body

        The water was cloud-green

                        but after it settled I found
        evidence of some sea animal

        whose very body was an organ it seemed, pre-classical

                            the calcium intestine fluted
as early Greek columns of poplars,
                        modest, empty.

            I tilt the glass and it picks up Pacific algae,

        her taste on my tongue

                        as I call anyone, my voice muffled

                by the rush of the river,

which splits this city, a creek really,

            with duck surfing sideways, glistening without effort—

Nightshade

I want to be lost outside this world,
                                        Rebekah

where the color of water is a window

                        outside the days

cut in the sheer of handmade
                                paper squares,

        each symmetrical and laid alongside
                                        in rows on a blank board,

the first assignment   they gave you   in art school.

        Color theory   immerses us in the chromas

                only to reveal

                        all color is only light,

                                        white before the sneeze,

            an accident of splitting

                        the atom or prism—

mysterious human eyes whose every tone is removed

                from

the simulacrum of the eye.

Now, I live in that prism of white.

A cousin to the willow curves
                    the gray light

of these two weeks of continuous, first
                              rain.

The green is alive   proliferating particles
                              of air

and I

    become them, the

    ravenous green of summer   split by the arid

                        California light,

    the shimmering greens of your face

                    as you move across canvas,

& the cool green of what blooms in the night

            —the delicate purple petals
                        each with a pale green vein
                bisecting the base.

INIMICAL TO THE TREES IN THIS WARM CLIME

stillness who had summer mint

dearest loss you suffer

wherein bitter change yourself

to the night spoon, this durable darkness

End of Summer

You are the beautiful
lip
against my nipple

but the red cup, a raspberry
is yours

speaking

you hold up your hand
an oracle perhaps

while I sleep on into the night
another monsoon or not

displaced from water to
this curtain of heat

long ago

the goats you tended
in New Mexico answered you

deep bleats and soft eyes meeting yours
their white bearded heads

and your palm above

my left breast, the heart

unmoving,

as the water moves out of the city
into the earth

White Noise

the invisibility of the squid whose chromatophores enlarge and
                                                        alter
in pursuit the dull side is for the lover the brilliant to suspend
                                                        belief
the chameleon has three-hundred sixty degrees and a prehensile
                                                        tale
we suppose the sustainability of the hand

the pupil enlarges during orgasm   squid die after birthing

food for Asteroidea

Very Large Array on earth resists exception

from the maritime view by night
diatom arrange by temperature
nocturnal stars below
—brittle, basket, snake, feather, necklace,
sea star, sea cucumber—swallowed
through water, their sound
& light
speak

The evolution of dusk into night
the silence of the day leaves me
an island in the darkness
light not as metaphor
but in sight

my own skin
reflects your eye
I could not have prepared for

In the constellation Hydra, whose brown dwarf star
shows a blue light in space
turned on or off in the vacuum
millennia light-years ago
a voice already dead once received transmits
the receiver our Earth
ocean basin of water
unique, alone & afloat

we hear the whssh of quiet nothing
where sound may not travel not singular
of carbon

Undressing the coast from flight
several ellipses of clouds suspend in the air
midway between window and water
the curved slice of Pacific
as if in negative land indistinguishable from the sea
both blue
the prism of atmosphere
colors my eyes
full of you I leave behind to the humid
glowing screens of your multiple tvs
as you edit and edit the film
tape already transferred
a body floats in the blueness
of pool water
my voice repeats words we believe
I submerged my head for the image
we were seeking of ourselves
was that it
a coast receding like the tide as I watch
you become only a speck
in your bedroom the door closed

Aquaria float across our mind's eye
a line
of glass boxes containing old dolls' heads, sharks,
Laminaria digitata, a spine, decaying books, a human leg, iridescent
jellyfish, green water, blue water

a film with assassinations, voices on loop for decades
as brilliant binary
chordata
waits to be found

in memory
one voice speaks out into space
is it you?
beautiful I

My stardust, my beloved

you began on the visible horizon before it existed

the universe's age is only as far as we can see

you cooled in envelopes of supergiants, listened

for the chemistry of *Planaria* in the elements in supernovae.

Red rust formations, blue-

green algae

in an ocean cooling to make

your beautiful flesh.

Redshift grows the distance you are away from me,

I turn red.

I am endemic to myself
when I have left for space 30 million light-years later
my voice which returns will find you dead
accept voice as light you see
accept my native flesh as solar fire, baryonic matter, dark
matter
bending the light,
dark energy.
Most is what we can't see not atoms
but an evidence of pull like desire,
a cosmological constant.
I will be remembered, a string
across the night sky
akin to lightning
but I am no more *real*
than you

The Future

This is what is meant by stars in the universe—

            they brush away the dust of my face

completely.
                  Orange Mars
                        blue Venus,

    we sleep as the dust of the mountain.

    What plants exist without us,

                  the wood we gather for the fire we make
              sleeps into the mountain for millennia

      this light contained only by stars or noctilucent insects

      no hominid made to make energy

                energy in our making.

The sky closes, a door into the darkness

        no more will remain than there

ever was.

           With this we sleep, my love and I.

White Goddess

How long you sleep
                    female without a head,

         head
                    piled sand   by a friend in capris.

Say the head is separate from the body.

On this shore (Pacific), I house bliss   drowning

                    languages,
                              squares whose perimeters do not
complete
         run ninety degrees drop

                              off the face,

reappear as rosebush in Chinatown balcony—

                    Fire lantern
                                   I grip your neck,

                                   not yet alive I

    while the poet lies beside you
                    caresses your ear, educates Sun

                                             I am the eye
                    the poet disinherits

Snow

The destination you follow along the edge of a sea

I take you to

a relief of waves against the pale, overcast sky

and sharp seagrass bisects the curve of my

shoulder hidden by the dunes

I did not ask for your name

you gave to me

a language learned after your native,

native

I am not home

when I return, transformed, you are alive

Deplaning the slope of stairs to the tarmac I catch the scent

seasonal plants

the French horizon clouded over

Take and surround me, don't pretend forgiveness

I know your mind,

hesitant and direct

Tell me what I will deny myself
as I have
my shoes make a sharp sound as I walk

around the side of the house, green shingles, north-facing
its door opens and closes behind you
beneath the bed I hide our intimacy

Suppose there is none
the train in the distance is our likeness
your hand on the small of my back
call my name or someone else's

To fly over the Atlantic
I have only one shoulder bag, jeans and a t-shirt
like Juliette Binoche
you've arrived, says the sign
I kiss no one

There is no snow here
a dead seabird, wet and grey
poetry I left because of sorrow

Neva

I'm not human for you, smallest side of a pin
whom I love. Summer in Boston. Water
of the lake, blue and cold at the bottom. Akhmatova
said the cold fire of the heart. I will quote her.
'Remember me'.

I am alive like the coathanger twisted for abortion.
That is not the truth, Akhmatova would say something
subtler, something about the mildness of the Neva
in winter, how her love is a shadow at dusk
moving across the sky, as it dies. My love
is not like that. I am like that

as I disappear.

A Concise History of the Female

"But please don't cry— …
Beauty does not rest."

—Anne Carson

What faith submits

my back a bridge for your feet

green ferns and day lilies over the pond

silver mirror and

inside the dark folds

smooth as stones,

the book

engages from suffering

Language unaccustomed from speech

malign me

I am not incremental

the flood as it imitates swallows

and I swallow but am not that

which is spoken of

grateful to be small

see the bodies as they float out to their graves

inside the tsunami

Her clitoris as it is cut out,
the light on the lintel as she is sewn
in the house of any village
sews my tongue
from the poem that breathes

In this urgency I speak to you, grieve,
make love—
the beautiful constellation of your brain
riding me into daybreak
a freedom past
unmanned bodies who have none, no sex left
have become liquid in the black dirt of a ditch
or only the words in my mouth,
speech through cotton

and I am somebody's wife but I am only
local
looking for my own
and I am no one's wife even
after ten years

Devotion does not ask for time,

the movements of trees and oceans.

What is gentle

the eye can answer without harm,

your hand on my back;

like fire in a metal can through the dark of night

on a city street—and homeless,

the new has been built

This darkness does not

will not be darkness as on Earth

we speak of the Sun, a god

and our orbit

one of isolation and fear

as if the coldness of space were itself cold, singular

and not just vacuum—

my hand outstretched in the winter air, chaffed

That which cannot be empty

I speak to

not divided but unremained

heat of stars and of energy

for there is nothing that protects us from passion

nor can there be

if we are to love like animals

beneath a Joshua Tree

and not eat each other

each limb chopped off and cooked for erasure

An excavation

two thousand years later reveals the bones

illuminated by yellow spotlights,

of Roman baths buried beneath a Medieval castle

in France,

each age consuming the previous,

then unearthed—

and would you not touch me

would you not love me if you could

decide

for humanity

Bee

The apiary inside me
                   is flush with bees.

   I fly into a field lit
                   by bells of blossoms,
                                        trees
         surveying, surveying

I was asleep,   a hard knot of fire and fur

         vibrating.

         Gold,   you are not hidden

among Mesquite, Prickly Pear,
            Saguaro, all the sources
of pollen
            I seek.

                   Beside the mind is heat,
the magma Bougainvillea.

   What is left is a hem of days,

                   undone by my own industry—
   But don't believe this voice.
                   Even human,

with hands

I cannot carry you.

Empty Map of Room

As time or poetry,   a silver nail on the wall
                                in the glint of dusk,
        glowing, alive.

Beside me, my body before the wall
                        as if touching
    the yellow light to my back.

  Love that is no more,   a glass of air

                    in the black
        of dusk.
                Behind me,

the wall behind you,   a frame
                            closes off.

Notes

Noctilucent
Noctilucent: Of or able to produce its own light or light source at night, glowing in the dark or with properties that allow it to glow in the dark; lighted at night.

kuanós: Sky, azure. Gr.

cyanic: Of the color blue corresponding to cyan, sky blue; like or of the blue of cyanide.

Archipelago
archipelago: The Aegean Sea; sea with numerous islands; group of many islands (*ODEE*, C.T. Onions, Ed.) The original breakdown of the Greek roots means "chief sea," from *arkhi-*, chief and *pélagos*, sea. Colloquial use by sailors in and around the Mediterranean cemented its present meaning of "a group of islands," by the general fact that the Aegean contained a large number of islands, which eventually led to the contemporary definition (*Arcade Dictionary of Word Origins*, John Ayto, Ed.).

domus: House or home, L.

Of Datura
Datura: A nightshade native to desert and liminal desert zones, having large pink-purple flowers, which blooms only at night.

Hildegard
Title refers to Hildegard von Bingen, composer, poet, playwright, herbalist, illustrator and nun.

Demotics
Demotic: Of ordinary people; demotic language or style (*OAD*, Eugene Ehrlich, Ed.).

driven mad, the sea: Edmond Jabès, *The Little Book of Unsuspected Subversion*, trans. Rosemarie Waldrop.

quanta: From quantum, 1. the amount required or desired 2. (in physics) a unit of quantity of energy proportional to frequency of radiation (*OAD*, Eugene Ehrlich, Ed.).

penumbra: The partly shaded region around the shadow of an opaque body, especially around the total shadow of the moon or Earth in eclipse (*OAD*, Eugene Ehrlich, Ed.).

senita: A desert flower.

ocotillo: A desert plant.

symbolon: Pieces of bone

desiccation: From desiccate—to make quite dry, to dry out the moisture from in order to preserve it (*OAD*, Eugene Ehrlich, Ed.).

diatom: A microscopic one-celled alga with a stony cell wall, existing in sea and fresh water and often forming fossil deposits (*OAD*, Eugene Ehrlich, Ed.).

dimorphic: Occurring in two distinct forms in the same species, individual, etc. (*OAD*, Eugene Ehrlich, Ed.)

all indivisible energy exists: Misprision of the definition of quantum physics, *Scientific American,* January, 2003.

ecliptic: The sun's apparent path among stars during the year (*OAD,* Eugene Ehrlich, Ed.).

anabasis: Military advance; ascent, walk-up (*ODEE,* C.T. Onions, Ed).

minimal amount of music...: From the liner notes of Górecki's *Symphony of Sorrowful Songs, Symphony No.3,* CD recording, Royal Philharmonic, London.

petrel: A kind of seabird that flies far from land (*OAD,* Eugene Ehrlich, Ed.).

lipstick pixie, fairy puke: The names of two varieties of epiphytic moss which grow in thick layers of dense forest indigenous to Pacific Northwest Temperate Rainforest zones.

epiphyte: A type of parasitic plant, fungi or other which attaches itself to and naturally grows on the exterior body of a host plant or tree.

perilune: The point in an object's orbit around the moon where it is closest to the moon's center (*OAD,* Eugene Ehrlich, Ed.).

water is why the epiphytes or guest plant: From an article on the geographical history of plants indigenous to the Pacific Northwest, *National Geographic Magazine,* Feb/March, 2003.

humans hate darkness...we had to light it: From an article on underwater photography *National Geographic Magazine,* Feb/March 2003.

Polis
References an article about the construction of the new subway in Greece, and the subsequent excavation of multiple layers of various Greek and Roman ages. The layers were partitioned off in Plexiglas throughout much of the subway system, allowing passengers to view their archeological history, as a sort of museum on either side of the train windows.

unloosening the stones of the Plaka: A public quarter in Athens renown for its popularity among tourists and locals for its nightlife.

thalassa-made: Thalassa – sea, Gr.

Lotus
In E.'s class: The poet, Eleni Sikelianos.

As If I Were Conceived in Her Diorama
someone has dialed my number: Olena Kalytiak Davis, *And Her Soul Out Of Nothing*.

what Stanislavsky taught: Constantin Stanislavsky, author of *An Actor Prepares*, a unique and radical text which formulated and established the theory of Method Acting.

sometimes you call up your own aphasia: From 'Another Underwater Conversation;' Olena Kalytiak Davis, *And Her Soul Out of Nothing*.

willful destruction of her texts: Of Sappho.

carbon-made: From the song 'Carbon,' by Tori Amos in *Scarlet's Walk*, CD, 2002.

Nightshade
Nightshade: Plant of genera Solanum and Atropa; any of several wild plants with poisonous berries or fruit having potentially narcotic properties (*OAD*, Eugene Ehrlich, Ed.).

White Noise
Asteroidea: A true starfish, a group in the phylum, Echinodermata.

Very Large Array: A radio astronomy observatory located in Socorro County, NM, U.S.A.

brittle, basket....sea cucumber: Names of different members of the phylum Echinodermata, the largest one to lack any freshwater or land representatives.

aquaria float across our mind's eye: Misprision of a lyric from the song 'Oceania' by Björk, *Medúlla*, CD, 2004.

White Goddess
Title refers to the book by the same name, by Robert Graves.

Acknowledgements

Grateful acknowledgment is made to following publications for poems that first appeared or are forthcoming in them.

A Trunk of Delirium: 'Bee,' 'Nightshade'
Blue Fifth Review: 'As If I Were Conceived in Her Diorama,' 'End of Summer,' 'Polis,' 'White Goddess'
Blue Fifth Review Chapbook Series No. 1 — The Body: 'Demotics'
Bombay Gin: Excerpt from 'Archipelago'
The Drunken Boat: 'Noctilucent,' 'Suffering'
Shearsman: 'A Concise History of the Female,' 'Hildegard,' 'Neva'
Sinister Wisdom: 'Epis'
Spiral Orb: 'The Future'

'As If I Were Conceived in Her Diorama,' was nominated for a Pushcart Prize and a Best of the Net Award, in 2007 and 2008.

I am grateful to the editors of these publications. Deep appreciation also to Brandeis University, Naropa University and Tucson-Pima Arts Council, for awards, grants, and the opportunity to have received my education. I am particularly grateful to my editor Tony Frazer for dedicated reading and design; to my teachers Olga Broumas, Eleni Sikelianos and Susan Dibble, who gave me poetry, dance and belief; to my parents in their generosity, Barbara and Harry Buckheit; to my sisters Lauren and Lindsey Buckheit; to Jacob Seiferle-Valencia, for his wisdom and honesty; to Anne Waldman; to Sandra Guzman, Paula Buckheit; to Rachel Lehrman, whose eyes and ears touched these poems from across the Atlantic; to Kobun Chino Roshi for his friendship; to my friends who have collaborated with and supported me in art, Eirikur Baldursson, Kathleen Barbosa, Lisa Cagnacci, Courtney Czar, Nathan Dryden, Jane Kohuth, Karyn Reim, Maria Sara Villa, Rebekah Wright, Jim Yagmin, Samantha Zirkin; to Jane Miller; Annie Brook; Esther Ratner; John Burt; Ernest Dodge; Sheila Johnson; Meg Files; Jackie M.; Zuzi! Dance community; Casa Libre; and with deepest love, particularly to Rebecca Seiferle, for the shared gift of poetry and life—thank you.

www.ingramcontent.com/pod-product-compliance
Lightning Source LLC
Chambersburg PA
CBHW031931080426
42734CB00007B/640